Sweet Thorns

Tara-Elizabeth Downs

BOOKMAN EXPRESS

Bookman Express, LLC
works@bookmanexpress.pub

ISBN: 9780985375560
LCCN: 2017956428

Cover art designed by Demi Walker.

For my grandmother.

To the girl

To the woman

To the boy

To the man

With flowers buried beneath their tongue

With soft in their touch

May these words find you

May they find you in peace

On a bright day or a still night

May they love you as they've loved me

May they heal you as they've healed me

May they be well to you

As they've done well for me.

Prologue

I'm alive. I'm a breathing, living, dancing thing. Every time I breathe, I come into myself and then release parts of me back into the Universe. This is how literature works, how it works for me; how poetry works, how it works for me. I walk into my writing and meet a different version of myself, then walk out whole, new, broken, full, fixed, empty and black. It is a different experience every time I write. This here, it is my breath, everything that makes me *me* in the simplest way possible.

Spine

Enigma

I am a mad woman protecting
cocooned evening dreams in the bosom.
A river overflowing
and running into itself.
A withering, weathering existence.
An ant.
A properly-homed gangster.
A bush woman carrying revolutions on my head
housing a room of breaths
that know no bounds.

Conformity

I am losing my tongue
and eating my stories again.
My words have gained too much weight
and are stuck at the back of my throat
refusing to leave my body.
I am wearing silence like the day now
wrapped in something looking like the good mannered
well behaved
skirt between legs
clasped hands in lap
speaks when spoken to
kind of woman.

Duty

Some of the women
who have made us
have stories still locked away in their gut.
In fists.
Stories that will never catch breath
nor grow body.
Stories that will never kiss the tongue
nor see light.
You must summon these stories out of them.

Elastic

How do I unbend my body
out of a question mark,
How do I breathe air through my spine,
How do I not see sores
on my skin,
bleeding goings,
How do I stitch my heart
back into the right kind of rose.

- the ongoing outs of insecurities

Are you a safe space?

Travel

What
kind of tongue do you wear
when you call home,
Do you remove your body before saying hello,
Do you take off your city before your mother's voice
comes on,
Are you afraid,
Do you tap your fingers on the counter anticipating the
voice from the other end,
Does it call you home,
Does it ask what kind of city foods you've been eating,
Does it ask for your husband,
Does it ask if you're pregnant yet,
Does it make you sad
this voice on the other end,
Are they why you don't call home often,
Do they tell you to call more often,
And come home
for God's sake
come home.

Mass

The bucket you carry on your head
every Wednesday morning
filled with dead weight
regrets
stinking molasses
and
leftover love.
Take it off
pour it under your feet
into the starved earth.

Let your face down
release the war from your fists
clean the sins from beneath your nails
give the day your shoulders
and begin again.

- **mental vacation**
self care

Aftermath

Forgive me
for I will come with my mouth full of fire
heated. blazing. burning. howling.
Forgive me
for I will come
carrying the ocean in the bottom of my belly
and I will pour. pour. pour.
Forgive me
for I am in love
and my heart is breaking
bursting
and
shrinking back into itself.

Grey Areas

I know I'm not your kind.
I know that you can only wear yourself.
That you are colour
and
shade.
That you have bandages beneath your shirt.
That your head is always in the ocean.
That you are never in your body.
I know that you want the feelings.
You want to stretch
and
hold air between your fingers.
I know you want to bend a little less.
It is easy to see you.
Anywhere.

Selfhood

The universe is moulding you in poised politeness.
There are dead lives living inside you
that you have not yet met.
There are years of becoming in your bones.
Watch the thorns kiss your skin
and walk into your becoming.
There is fire brewing in your eyes, sister.
Protect it.
Nurture it.

You are young love
and
you are my prayer.

- love notes on high tides

Irony

They say God is supposed to save us
but I sometimes believe
this energy might be the devil
spitting fire in our faces.

The Breaking

I do not enjoy my heart
being dragged out of my chest
on days when I want only
to breathe in bloom
and sing to the sky.

Such magic you are,
making my heart explode
inside my chest
like dancing symphonies
in a cloudless sky.

- a corn-starched love poem

Red

I still do not know why
my uterus has to choke on fire
roll on a field of thorns
bleed and die
just to birth fiery gods.

Temporary

I cannot move in.
I have to continue living
on the edge of love,
on the edge of life
with my bags packed.
Life is a glass table.

Grey Areas II

There is a breathing boy somewhere
around here.
I want to weave her pain into a poem.
I want to take her skirt off
to tell her story,
to call her out of him.
I want to call her out of him.

Colour

I loved a woman.
This is how it began.
I loved a woman.
This is how it ended.

Prickle

Colour II

It is sad how you forced us
to deny ourselves.
Deny ourselves
until what's left of us
is living in shadows.

Weight

Sometimes
mornings ambush me
and days feel like extra luggage
I'm too weak to carry.

Strength

There have been days
when there were no colours
no light in my cheeks
no spunk in my eyes
no laughter in my belly.

There have been days
rainy. wet. cold. dark.
Days when
my voice cracks
and Earth is mean.
When
walls are closing in
and the sky is angry.

There have been such days
but here I am
black and alive.
Here I am
with oil betwixt my lips
honey on my teeth.

Here I am, shivering, smiling.
I have survived the storm.

Age

You must have rhythm
left in your bones.
It is the aftermath of grief.

Motion

Teach me
how to walk out of my body
and let it breathe.
Then
teach me how
to walk back into myself
and stay.

3 O'clock Musings

Perhaps
it is easier to make ourselves swallow the
handicapped letters
resembling truth
at half past three in the morning
when the blank spot inches away from our thighs
screams at us
and the demons are still roaming red within.

Knees

When
the darkness and the wildness
of the night
explode in me
I kneel on my side
and pray for the rain to touch me elsewhere,
for her to soak the parts of me
that aren't blistered.
The parts that aren't folding in on themselves.

Melodies

I want
the kind of love
that will fall into the bath tub
and disco my bones.

Courage

Sister,
you are bleeding in and out.
Why not move your heart
from your lover's hand
and watch splinters vanish.

Struggle

Some days
I do not try to find God in soft prayers.
Some mornings
I do not search for answers full of light.
When I rise, I do not always find the sun.
I have to dig my way from hell
with my tongue
buried in my back.

Garden

I'm still in bloom
still shedding
petal by petal.
Still breathing in the sun
and gasping for air.
Water me.

Options

You can either learn to hug your sins
or let them dig into you
turning your insides black
driving you off the edge.

Room

I hope this tiny home will always
hold you upon entry.
May it become the birth place of dreams
and a cushioned nest
for your mighty heart.

Expanding

There is a hum in the centre of my ribs
in the midst of my lungs
at the back of my throat
and, steady,
it swells and grows
and I'm living in crescendo.

Tongues

When you give me words
from the head
from the moment,
the kind that fills me
that makes me safe,
the kind that tricks me
that makes me smile,
I will not tell you I know.
I will take them
paste them on my skin
and let myself feel.
I will tell myself to feel your lies
how beautiful they look on my skin.

Gone

You have become a fleeting grey
budding in the middle of my head
like hot, black blood
brewing beneath a punctured thumb.
You are cold sea water
and
broken notes.
The sweet pieces
of freshly broken splinters
sticking in the flesh.
You loved me in.

You are not a chore.
You are no one's duty.
You are not exhausting.
Stop letting them
puncture you with their hands.
You do not need stitching.
You need water.
Water yourself.

- **for girls like me**

Thorn

Home

Even though I had been gone for more than a decade, as soon as I crawled up the driveway of my childhood home, things were just the way they should be. Exactly how I'd left them. The heads of the quailed, pink roses were still peeking through the edges of the window sill beneath my grandmother's "prayer room" and the fowl coop still smelled a little rancid from just a foot away.

Our cat Betty is with child again and grandfather's pot belly has shrunk just a little bit. "Bwoy T, dem doctors know wah dem a say. Mi did need fi tek off some a di weight." He tilted his head and grinned at me, boyishly. He is such a sweet, kind man.

I parked up in the half alive garage, jumped out of my second-hand garden jeep and inhaled deeply as I took a good look around our yard. This is home. It still smells like a freshly cooked Sunday morning breakfast and Red Stripe beer, and the sun is still eating away the morning dew on the veranda steps. It is clean, except for Betty's muddy paws, scattered on soiled, ancient tiles.

My room still reeks of cinnamon, baby powder and doll hair and three sized-four, dry, rotten pairs of boots are still sitting neatly at the foot of my bed. Grandma never gave them away, just in case I'd want them.

Everything still sits. Just the way I left them. The big brilliant Zimbabwean painting still stands in the living room, right next to the Jesus mural that marks "African Leopard, Zimbabwe."

I remember feeling so smart that I was able to read that and pronounce *Zimbabwe* at 6 years old.

Maas Thompson still owns the meat shop and his fruit stall at the side of the road, and Bredda Leon is still running Tara Courier jokes. Timothy down the road still has a lisp, Jimmy is still begging "a likkle smalls" and teefing bwoy Sam-Sam is still stealing jackfruits and apples from our backyard.

It's all the same, still, and I'm enjoying it.

Papa is definitely stirring something in the kitchen. It smells like steamed cabbage and fried dumplings with cornmeal and bissy tea. I feel centred. I feel loved. I feel every light and sweet thing creeping back inside me.

All is well right now. I'm home.

Culture

Saturday evenings at the hairdresser shop used to always be a show. My grandmother would take me to get my hair done for Sunday morning church service, Sunday School and school Monday morning. Saturday was always my favourite day of the week. When else would I learn how Aunty Marlene caught Susan from down the road sucking tongues with Junior roun' by the church back? That's Miss Vera's last boy who is married to Jacqueline Samuels, the one white lady in the community.

Saturdays were the only time I would ever see Grandma's best friend, Evangelist Marcia hold her belly and grin like she's 16 with a new crush on the brown boy at the back of the class. She is always so serious, like she's kneading centuries of pain in her body.

This particular Saturday, while Aunty Roxanne's daughter, Sasha combed my hair into tiny plaits, she whispered, like all the adults do when they're about to chat other people's business, "Cover yuh ears, cah you is likkle pickney an' a big people argument dis."

Of course I would cover my ears, but just for show, because my little 10-year-old self needed to find out what Sister Lorna did when Pastor Fairway found out she was teefin' money from the church vestry to go obeah man in St. Mary.

A Disapproval of Skimpy Things

My brother doesn't look at me anymore. He looks past me, over me. I think he's afraid of the chaos that's growing on my face.

He says I don't look the same anymore and I can't tell whether his voice is washed with concern, disdain, or pain. He says he prays for me, that one day I will find God and a good husband, and I will find my place in the church, *"where you belong,"* he says. He says I look like *"those kinds of people"* with my hair *"shaved like that."* The kinds of people, he means, who are brave enough to own themselves.

He cannot look me in the eyes. So he stares past my shoulder when he asks what I had to eat. He digs nervously at the top of his head and asks the edge of my shoulder when am I going to start wearing *"decent"* clothes, eyeing my ripped jeans shorts nesting on the edge of my thighs. He says I don't look like a child of God and that makes him sad.

My brother doesn't look at me anymore because he thinks I'm lost. He doesn't recognize the stretched out energies floating around in this host of a body. He says it breaks him that I've lost the church.

My brother doesn't look at me anymore because I've started carrying too much colour, too much rebellion, too much expression, in all the places too hot for him to hold.

Richard

This was about girlfriend number eight or so, I dunno. I had lost count. I liked the one before her though. She had dimples and it was always an interesting show to see her lips part and her cheeks abandon her soft brown face every time she smiled. She was nice. I preferred her. She liked me too, you know. She'd bring me kiss cakes and other little fancies.

I stuffed my short chubby thumb in my mouth and shifted my shoulders to lean on my grandfather's knees as I watched my big brother introducing his new girlfriend to the family. My grandfather and I exchanged knowing looks because we knew this wouldn't be his last, poor girl.

I wasn't sure if I liked this new one. Her skin was lighter than my kiss cake friend with the dimples and she was as tall as an alien. I didn't like her very much as a matter of fact. Plus, she gave me nothing. I thought she'd know that the only way to an 8-year-old's heart was through her sweet tooth. Shame on her. I was determined not to be her friend.

Mother

I'm 6 years old. Mommy came to visit yesterday. She just showed up, can you imagine? I was busy though. Grandmother was having another of her pigs killed, I don't quite remember if that pig was mine. Grandmother used to always give me a pig.

Anyway, she just showed up, with my brother and sister at her side. The yard was full, yet I was able to spot her from a mile away - well, not literally but you get the point.

I ran! I ran! Very fast. As fast as I could. As soon as I spotted her, I dropped my roasted pig meat and bolted through the gate with my thousand hair accessories slapping against my skull. It hurt but I didn't care. That was my mother out there.

I leaped into her arms. She asked if I was okay. I nodded with so much enthusiasm. Why wouldn't I be? My mother was here and I was in her arms.

Flashback

My mother is the parched yellow skin woman with the long, red nail-polished fingers. My father is the thick, short, dark brown, briefcase gentleman who dashed past me at 8 o'clock this morning, with spectacles bouncing off the edge of his nose.

And me, I'm still that 12-year-old girl with the chiney bumps and dodo plaits dangling from my head. Too lonely for love. Too lost for myself and still waiting on salvation from the sun.

Prodigal Sister

It is quarter to nine and I just pulled out my laundry bag to get started on my load when I saw that you had gotten married yester evening.

Facebook said you were in France and, bwoy, from the looks of it, you did get some rotten wealthy guy to kiss your feet and blow rainbow marks from your ass.

You got it!

And, I just wanted to ask you, how are you in France, slapping life where it hurts, while your dead grandmother turns blue underneath a white, bloody sheet in a funeral home halfway across the world.

Holiday

You must breathe sometimes too.
You deserve it.
Stand on your bed and inhale the air from your top bedside
window.
Put some music on and take a bath.
Dance.
Let the music sway you.
Let the strings of the instruments love your bones.
You should cry sometimes too
then laugh at yourself because you know how ugly your face
looks when it breaks for the pain.
Call a friend – tell them you're losing weight.
Tell them you've cooked today
and that you ran 5 miles this morning
even though it's a lie
but you must exaggerate a little.
Tell your 60-year-old neighbour good morning.
Offer to water her plants when she leaves for her doctor's
appointment tomorrow morning.
Tell your baby brother he is beautiful.
Kiss your mother's stomach.
Put some flowers on Aunt Patsy's balcony across the street.
Live a little
and breathe.
You are allowed.
You have earned the right.
You must remember this,
Friend.
Sister.
Son.
Breathe.

- a note to all of us

Acknowledgements

To all the energies of light and strength that have helped me along my journey of being.

To everyone who has contributed to this project.

I thank you hard and heavy.

NOTES // REFLECTIONS

www.ingramcontent.com/pod-product-compliance
Lightning Source LLC
Chambersburg PA
CBHW051739040426
42447CB00008B/1214